DO YOU SOMETIMES NEED TO SWEAR BUT CAN'T?

DOES IT ANNOY THE SHITAKE MUSHROOM OUT OF YOU?

WELL THEN THIS BOOK IS PERFECT!

EACH PAGE IN THIS BOOK HAS A RELAXING MANDALA CONTAINING A CLEAN SWEAR WORD THAT YOU CAN USE AS OFTEN AS YOU LIKE!

HAPPY COLORING!

ISBN-13: 978-1986928687
ISBN-10: 1986928683

COLORING CREW

COLORING CREW

COLORING CREW

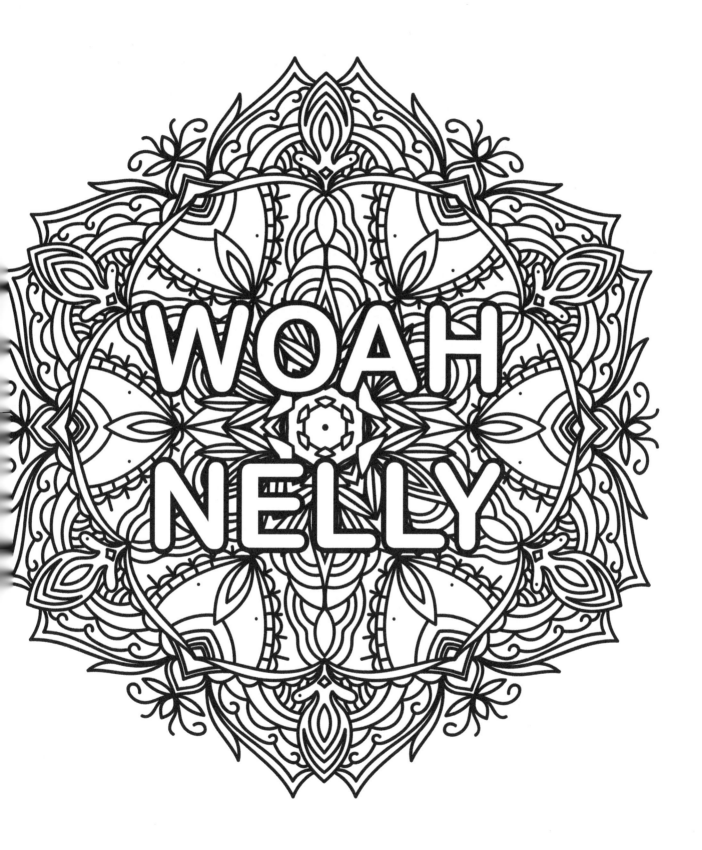

COLORING
CREW

COLORING CREW

COLORING CREW

COLORING
CREW

COLORING CREW

COLORING CREW

COLORING CREW

COLORING CREW

COLORING CREW

COLORING CREW

COLORING CREW

COLORING
CREW

COLORING CREW

COLORING CREW

COLORING CREW

COLORING CREW

COLORING
CREW

COLORING CREW

COLOR TEST
PAGE

COLORING CREW

THANKS!
WE HOPE YOU HAD FUN!

IF YOU LIKED THIS BOOK THEN YOU YOU CAN
VIEW OUR FULL RANGE OF HILARIOUS ADULT
COLORING BOOKS BY GOING TO AMAZON AND
SEARCHING FOR "COLORING CREW" AND THEN
CLICKING ON OUR AUTHOR PAGE.

THANKS AGAIN!

COLORING CREW

Made in United States
North Haven, CT
08 December 2021

12164244R00026